The Triduum and Easter Sunday
Breaking Open the Scriptures

John J. Pilch

D1502357

A Liturgical Press Book

THE LITURGICAL PRESS
Collegeville, Minnesota

1	2	3	4	5	6	7	8

Library of Congress Cataloging-in-Publication Data

Pilch, John J.
   The Triduum and Easter Sunday : breaking open the Scriptures / John J. Pilch.
     p. cm.
   ISBN 0-8146-2727-7 (alk. paper)
   1. Paschal triduum—Liturgy—Texts—History and criticism. 2. Easter—Liturgy—Texts—History and criticism. 3. Bible—Social scientific criticism. 4. Bible—Homiletical use. I. Title.

BX2015.785 P55 2000
264'.02034—dc21   99-088080

Contents

Introduction

During the last decade or two it became popular to speak about "Breaking Open the Scriptures." No one seems to remember who originated the phrase, and interpretations of it vary. The image, however, is constant. The Scriptures are not self-evident to the Western reader. Rather, they require informed assistance and serious study in order to be understood.

One summer, a young Christian bishop from Baghdad, Iraq, was enrolled in my graduate course at the University of San Francisco entitled "Introduction to the Cultural Context of the Old Testament." It soon became clear to the other students that he had an advantage. He perceived and identified Middle Eastern cultural elements in the Bible that completely eluded the notice of the Western students. On the other hand, he had no interest in or awareness of the historical setting of the texts, something of keen interest to the Western students, even if they struggled to master dates from 2000 years B.C.E. His entire education about the Bible to that point had been in the interpretation of the Bible produced by the Fathers of the Church, especially the Eastern Fathers. Since those interpretations were rarely if ever "historical-critical" but rather "spiritual," the bishop's preaching centered only on the "spiritual" interpretation of the Bible applicable to all people of all times. For all the students in this class, then, the Scriptures definitely needed to be "broken open."

In this booklet we approach the Triduum readings according to the same principles used by the architects of the Lectionary when they selected and arranged the readings. We begin with the gospel in order to gain a firm grasp of the meaning intended by the Evangelist. Next we turn to the first reading since, in general, the architects of the Lectionary operated on a principle of "harmony." Such harmony is most evident when the doctrine or event reported in the New Testament bears a more or less explicit correlation with the Old Testament reading. The second reading often has no relationship to the first and third. On the Sundays of the year, the second readings form a semi-continuous sequence mainly from the writings of the apostles. This is a summary of the rationale for selecting the readings for the Triduum which the architects of the Lectionary present in chapter V, paragraph #4, of the *Introduction to the Lectionary*. In this booklet we present the Middle Eastern cultural background information necessary for "breaking open" these Scriptures.

The readings from the Bible assigned in the Lectionary for the Triduum pose special challenges. The Gospel of John is prominent, and the Greek word he uses which is translated "Jews" in English is particularly problematic. The growing consensus among modern Jewish and Christian scholars is that the English word "Jews" is anachronistic. Since contemporary Judaism and modern Jewish beliefs and practices are rooted in the formation of the Talmud in the fifth century C.E., the English word "Jew" should not be used when referring to events before that time. Indeed, the Greek word used by John literally means "Judean" and describes not only the people living in Judah or Judea but all who worshiped the God of Israel whose temple was in Jerusalem in Judea. In this booklet I use the words "Judaic," "Judean," and "Israelite."

Though the word "Israelite" originally described people of the northern kingdom (921–721 B.C.E.), it was eventually appropriated by the southern kingdom so that it is historically appropriate for the entire period of First Temple Judaism: 950 B.C.E. to 586 B.C.E. In Matthew's Gospel, of course, Jesus calls his ethnic group *the house of Israel* (10:6; 15:24), and the followers of Yoḥanan ben Zakkai (c. 70 C.E.), who are usually called "rabbis," refer to their group as *Israel* well into Talmudic times. (See "Jews and Christians," in my *The Cultural Dictionary of the Bible* [The Liturgical Press, 1999]). Preachers and liturgy planners, therefore, will have to learn an entirely new way of thinking and speaking as they compose homilies and prayers which involve this terminology.

Another feature commonly associated with "Breaking Open the Scriptures" is an interest in deriving relevance for today's life from the Bible. Such a desire is completely understandable and intelligible, yet fraught with difficulty. In their 1987 *Pastoral Statement for Catholics on Biblical Fundamentalism*, the Bishops of the United States cautioned against "an effort to try to find in the Bible *all the direct answers for living*" (emphasis added) because the Bible itself nowhere claims such authority. Preachers, liturgy planners, musicians and lyricists, and ordinary readers of the Bible all must exercise great caution in their attempts to make the Scriptures "relevant." The task is not impossible, but it is much more difficult than most people realize.

A common rule of thumb among many biblical scholars is that in order to know what the text **means** (for us today), it is imperative to know what it **meant** (for the original author and the original audience). Phrased differently, it is impossible to say what the text means unless one knows what it meant. In this booklet I have sought to explain first and foremost what each individual text-segment meant for the original author. Vatican II's Document on Revelation phrased it thus: "In order to see clearly what God wanted to communicate to us, [the interpreter of sacred Scripture] should carefully investigate what meaning the sacred writer really intended, and what God wanted to manifest by means of their words" (#12).

Further, seeking to discover the relevance and applicability of ancient documents from the Mediterranean culture for contemporary Western cultural contexts is a challenge of mammoth proportions. It is a matter of cross-cultural communication, never an easy task. Fortunately an ever increasing number of excellent resources exist that seek to explain what the Scriptures **meant**. In addition to *The Cultural Dictionary of the Bible* already mentioned, another mini-dictionary is available: *Biblical Social Values: A Handbook*, edited by John J. Pilch and Bruce J. Malina (Peabody, Mass.: Hendrickson Publishers, 1998). Both books contain extensive references to additional resources. Two commentaries specifically sensitive to the Mediterranean cultural context of the Gospels by Bruce J. Malina and Richard L. Rohrbaugh are noteworthy: *Social Scientific Commentary on the Synoptic Gospels* (Minneapolis: Fortress Press, 1992); and *Social Scientific Commentary on the Gospel of John* (Minneapolis: Fortress Press, 1998).

Determining what the Scripture might **mean** for the modern reader is matter of cross-cultural communication and interpretation. The method involves three steps. First, the interpreter must know her or his own culture very well and very critically (e.g., the United States). "Critical" knowledge of one's culture is objective, reflexive, and comparative at the very least. Personal experience, the favorite American "sample of one" ("I"), or the results of contemporary opinion polls are an inadequate basis on which to build a critical understanding of one's culture. *American Cultural Patterns: A Cross-Cultural Perspective* by Edward C. Stewart and Milton J. Bennet (Yarmouth, Me.: Intercultural Press, 1992) is a handy and brief book to help an interpreter get started in this part of the task.

Second, the interpreter must know the alien culture equally well and critically (the Middle Eastern world in which the Bible originated). Information about the Middle Eastern cultural world of the present and antiquity has been integrated by biblical scholars in the books mentioned above. For an extensive list of resources, consult John H. Elliott, *What is Social-Scientific Criticism?* (Minneapolis: Fortress Press, 1993).

Third, the interpreter must build a bridge between the cultures. This is essentially what preachers, liturgists, musicians, and lyricists must do. This is the heart of cross-cultural communication, and the rich resources of that discipline are invaluable for this step of the process. The publications of David Augsburger, a pastoral care specialist, offer good examples to imitate (*Pastoral Counseling Across Cultures* [Louisville: Westminster John Knox Press, 1986]; *Conflict Mediation Across Cultures* [Louisville: Westminster John Knox Press, 1992]).

Only with a tested and replicable process for cross-cultural communication such as this can the Scriptures really be broken open. This booklet and its companions (*The Cultural World of Jesus Sunday by Sunday*, 3 vols.; *The Cultural Dictionary of the Bible*) attempt to help build that bridge.

John J. Pilch
September 17, 1999
Feast of the Stigmata of St. Francis of Assisi

1

Holy Thursday

Readings:
John 13:1-15
Exodus 12:1-8, 11-14
1 Corinthians 11:23-26

John 13:1-15

John's account of the Last Supper does not report the institution of the Eucharist but does include a foot-washing during the meal, an action which has no precedent in any Judaic meal-ritual of this time! What does it mean?

In the Mediterranean world people communicate both in word and in deed. In this culture, actions often speak louder than words. This particular washing of the feet is clearly understood in the culture as a "symbolic action," that is, a deed that not only represents reality but effectively sets it in motion or a deed that propels an already initiated event still further forward toward completion. Prophets like Jeremiah (e.g., 13:1-11) and Ezekiel (e.g., 4) performed symbolic actions which to non-Mediterranean people look very much like bizarre behavior.

Notice that Jesus performs his symbolic action after the devil convinces Judas to betray Jesus (13:2). The devil tests

Judas' loyalty to Jesus, and sadly Judas yields and proves disloyal (13:27). Jesus' symbolic action thus further propels forward toward completing an event, Jesus' death, which has already been initiated by Judas' willingness to betray Jesus.

Jesus' symbolic action receives two interpretations in the text (vv. 1-11, 12-20). In the first interpretation the allusions to Jesus' approaching death in verses 1-3 indicate that Jesus' washing of the disciples' feet, on one level, signifies his humiliating death on their behalf (see 10:11, 15; 18:12-14). Verse 10 makes it even clearer, especially if the phrase "except for the feet" could be omitted in this Lectionary reading as it is in ancient manuscripts and in the New Jerusalem Bible translation. Then the "bathing" would implicitly refer to the foot-washing, and the reader or listener can understand why Jesus rejects Peter's request for additional washings (head and hands), or washing of the entire body.

On another level, the washing of the feet points to another symbolism. Streets in antiquity were filled with human and animal waste. A person walking the streets inevitably had soiled and smelly feet. Washing the feet of guests was usually a task for slaves or low-status servants. That Jesus would do a slave's task stuns his disciples. But they are missing his primary intended symbolic meaning which is more than humility.

In biblical times people considered the hands and feet as a zone of the human body symbolizing human activity. To wash the feet (or hands) is to wash away the offensive deeds performed by these appendages. Foot-washing is therefore equivalent to forgiveness. When Jesus urges them to repeat this action, he is not urging them to wash feet but rather to forgive each other as he forgives them. The end result of such mutual forgiveness, of course, is greater group cohesion and solidarity. This, in fact, is what Jesus is building here.

Verses 12-20 explicitly state the second interpretation of the foot-washing that is already implied in the preceding verses (hands-feet zone). Jesus gives his disciples an example to imitate among one another. They are to forgive one another and create strong bonds of fellowship. (1 Tim 5:10 indicates how seriously this example was followed particularly by widows.) This interpretation receives fuller explanation in John 15:12-13 where loving one another includes willingness to lay down life for one another. Thus foot-washing, even in this second interpretation, retains a relationship with the death of Jesus and the community that he strengthened on the night before he died.

A Mediterranean cultural perspective on this text offers at least two insights. The first insight derives from the meals in this cultural world. In the Middle East, unrelated people rarely if ever eat together. Meals are shared only with relatives. A stranger taken into a Mediterranean family is also temporarily transformed into a friend in order to be able to share the family meal. But groups in the Middle East, such as the Twelve, are surrogate-kinship groups—that is, they are just like family. Thus Jesus' symbolic action of foot-washing and its obvious (to those original viewers) reference to his death, to forgiveness, and to group cohesion would not be lost on the disciples. Eating a meal with Jesus renders one a family member, and family members willingly sacrifice for other family members.

(Parenthetically, this cultural insight explains Paul's ire when Peter ceases to eat with uncircumcised Galatian converts who accepted Jesus as Messiah [Gal 2:11-21]. Paul had to remind the Galatians that Peter's fickle behavior should not shake their confidence in being able to truly and meaningfully call God "Father." Having received the Spirit, they are truly part of God's family in spite of the false message Peter's non-verbal behavior communicates: that they are not family, or even surrogate-family members.)

The second insight to be gained by reading this passage from a Mediterranean cultural perspective concerns the uniquely Middle Eastern understanding of *humility*. In the Mediterranean world, a humble person never presumes to overstep bounds but rather deliberately stays at least one step behind to avoid creating even an impression of pretending to be more than one truly is. Mediterranean people derive status from birth and never try to improve that status. The culture forbids it. For this reason, a Mediterranean person understates actual status to be certain not to step beyond it, or even to create that impression.

This is quite in contrast with the Western understanding of humility, which generally means absence of self-assertion. The "humble" Westerner does not proclaim personal worth but also does not deny compliments when they are given. Further the Westerner never takes a step below status so that others might point to the rightful status. This contrasts with Jesus the "humble" Mediterranean person who protested "Don't call me good!" when he was addressed in this way by a respectful admirer (Mark 10:18). Here are two culturally different ways of being humble illustrated by one's attitude toward personal status.

Exodus 12:1-8, 11-14

As it stands in our current Lectionary, this reading from Exodus derives from the Priest-tradition ("P") of the Torah which presents the "rubrics" or liturgical directives regarding the proper observance (vv. 1-8) and the "historicized" significance of the feast of Passover (vv. 11-14). The Priest-tradition is concerned with rekindling in the people of their day (sixth century B.C.E.) the very same openness and enthusiasm as displayed by their ancestors on the day of their deliverance. Notice the urgency of personal involvement and participation reflected in verse 11.

Historically, two feasts were conflated into the feast of Passover: a nomadic, springtime rite involving blood to insure fecundity of the flock and to ward off evil by smearing the blood on tent poles and an agricultural harvest feast observed in the eating of unleavened bread. Notice that today's reading relates only the nomadic elements featuring lamb and blood.

This reading assigned for Holy Thursday is deliberately linked with the Johannine Jesus, the sacrificial lamb, whose blood gains salvation for all. In John, Jesus dies on the feast of Passover at the moment the lambs are being sacrificed for the festal meal. The Hebrew word for Passover, *Pesah*, is also the name of the nomadic springtime feast which became historicized in the Exodus experience when God "passed over" (see v. 13—"I will pass over"—*pesahti* in Hebrew) the homes whose lintels had been covered with the blood of the lamb.

Viewed from a Mediterranean cultural perspective, some simple verses in today's reading stand out more starkly and reverberate in modern Western minds with some shock. In the Mediterranean world, men eat alone and separately, women and children including males younger than the age of puberty eat earlier and separately. According to Gen 18:9, Sarah was not present at the meal Abraham served to the strangers. Exod 12:3-4 directs that "every man" shall take a lamb for the household, and if the household is too small then include the neighboring household for this feast. And again in Exod 12:24 one reads that "you shall observe this rite as an ordinance for you and for your sons for ever." Recall also the gospel stories of multiplication of loaves (Mark 6:35-44 and par.; Mark 8:1-10 and par.) among which only Matthew adds to the number 4,000/5,000 the phrase: "besides women and children." The groups of fifty into which the crowd was divided were same-gender groups, segregated in public by gender just as they are in Mediterranean households of antiquity and certainly in the Bedouin present. (For a photograph of a Mediterranean-style "family picnic" see http://www.georgetown.edu/faculty/pilchj, click on Mediterranean culture, "Gender-divided society.")

On the basis of modern Jewish custom, some scholars have argued that if Jesus "ordained" priests at the Last Supper, women had to be included because they were needed to light the candles for this feast. Such a hypothesis has no Mediterranean cultural plausibility where to this day Mediterranean peasant men and women eat (and sleep!) separately. The candle lighting ritual of the contemporary meal is a medieval element and is not found in any of the traditional texts (Torah, Mishnah, Talmud).

Preachers will, of course, be sensitive to history and tradition in constructing their homily for this occasion. One need not be an antiquarian purist, but one must also maintain a responsible sense of historical development and be keenly aware of the complex relationship between the many elements of our liturgical celebrations which derive from different centuries.

1 Corinthians 11:23-26

The Corinthian Christian community is probably one of the better known of all the early communities. The verses selected for today's feast are torn from their larger context (11:17-34) in order to highlight Paul's interpretation of the institution of the Eucharist (verses 23-27).

Drawing upon a favorite literary pattern among the ancients, A B A', Paul notes division and lack of unity at the very celebration that is supposed to effect unity (A: vv. 17-22). Jesus' Eucharist should serve a very different purpose (B: vv. 23-27). Disrespectful and shameful celebration of this sacrament carries its own penalty in its wake (A': vv. 28-34).

By carving verses 23-26 away from their total context for today's liturgy, the architects of the Lectionary intend that Paul should supply what is lacking in today's gospel: an account of the institution of the Eucharist.

Paul's account is the earliest of all accounts, even though it is similar to Luke 22:19-20. Paul adds "do this in remembrance of me" over the cup as over the bread, and he adds "which is for you" to the words "This is my body."

For Paul the Eucharist is a concrete occasion of Christ's presence in and unity with his people. It is also a memorial of his salvific death as described in John's Gospel for today, and the celebration of Eucharist must continue until he returns. These verses from Paul and the selection from John's Gospel for today's feast present to modern-day believers an understanding of Jesus' Last Supper as found in divergent (!) early traditions: the Pauline and the Johannine. Genuine respect for our ancestors in the faith will surely guide the preacher and liturgical planners to respect the uniqueness of each. The preacher will no doubt blend aspects of the traditions into a personal theological synthesis, a common feature in all preaching. It is best to identify this as a *personal* synthesis.

Suggestions for the Homilist

The preacher is challenged to integrate a number of themes: the Passover, the Eucharist, and the foot-washing, with their respective meanings. Some may enjoy taking detours through history, and others may prefer efforts at modernizing or contemporizing ancient traditions. These are normal and praiseworthy Western interests.

Perhaps the feast is best observed by remembering that Jesus rather than the Eucharist or the foot-washing is the focus of the Passover symbolism conveyed in today's readings. Jesus is, of course, connected with all three themes of the day. Indeed, relating the blood of Jesus, the Johannine lamb of God, with the paschal lamb of Exodus is one of the rare instances in the liturgy where the gospel does not have to be a supercessionistic reading of the Old Testament. (Supercessionism is a jargon-word describing a conviction by some Christians that the Old Testament has value *only* as it is fulfilled and surpassed in the New Testament.) It is sufficient to note a common, Mediterranean cultural tradition that repeats itself even in modern times.

Moreover, focusing on the distinctiveness of symbolic action in Mediterranean culture, the preacher might be able to switch attention from the superficial fact that only men's feet were washed to the meaning of the fact: all followers of Jesus are expected to be forgive one another, form cohesive community, and be willing to sacrifice—even life—for others.

Focusing on symbolic action and attempting to relate its significance to the contemporary United States, the preacher might invite worshipers to reflect upon their own distinctively individualistic and American decisions and actions that they have initiated in their lives and that continue to move their destiny forward toward fulfillment. In America we believe we have control over our lives and can change or reshape our destinies. Perhaps today's feast gives us an opportunity to do that.

Historical-Pastoral Reflections

Holy Thursday is a Johnny-come-lately day in Holy Week. It was first in the fourth century that Good Friday and Pascha emerged as feasts. In the fifth century St. Ambrose used foot-washing as a post-baptismal gesture for newly baptized at the Easter Vigil. For Holy Thursday, imitation of Jesus' foot-washing appears to have emerged in the seventh century, though it was not until the monastic liturgies of the eleventh and twelfth centuries that it became a general practice throughout the West and gradually spread to the cathedrals. The Last Supper commemoration first appears in the eighth century.

1. Given this relatively "late" development of Holy Thursday, how do you view contemporary adaptations such as replacing foot-washing (of some men) with hand-dipping (of all present)? Or the inclusion of women and children among the candidates for foot-washing?

2. How can the humiliating salvific death of Jesus, or mutual forgiveness, or community formation associated with foot-washing be transferred to another symbol?

3. Take the opportunity to discuss cultural differences relative to meals as noted in the commentary above. How might modern Western believers respect these ancient traditions while remaining true to their own cultural identity and traditions?

2

Good Friday

> **Readings:**
> John 18:1–19:42
> Isaiah 52:13–53:12
> Hebrews 4:14-16; 5:7-9

John 18:1–19:42

The repeated and strong emphasis upon Jesus' divinity together with the triumphalist tone in John's version of the Passion read on Good Friday blunt the shock of the Synoptic versions which are read on Palm Sunday in each cycle.

My favorite literary analysis of John's Gospel and his Passion Narrative is a long-standing one recently refined by Bruce J. Malina and Richard L. Rohrbaugh in their *Social Science Commentary on the Gospel of John* (Minneapolis: Fortress Press, 1998). I have modified their outline, though our analysis of the central scene is nearly identical. Such an analysis is rooted in the fact that artists (speakers, writers, composers) create their works by using patterns or structures that help an attentive reader or listener to follow and grasp the artist's intended meaning. In his *Magnificat* J. S. Bach used a form of concentric musical composition so that when the singers arrive at the words "As it was in the beginning . . ." that musical pattern repeats the pattern from the beginning of his composition. Musically at the end of his composition, Bach reminds the listener how it was "musically" at the beginning.

In similar fashion, the author of John's Gospel favors clusters of seven. For instance, he reports just seven signs (which the Synoptics call mighty deeds) during the ministry of Jesus. In any literary composition where seven items stand out, it is possible to view them in "step progression" or in "concentric arrangement." Jesus' dialogue with the Samaritan woman (John 4) is an example of "step progression." Jesus and the woman speak to each other seven times. In the woman's seven responses to Jesus, she gives evidence of a progressively improving understanding of who Jesus really is: Judean, Sir (*Kyrie*), Prophet, Messiah. In the end she becomes the first "evangelizer" in John's Gospel: "many Samaritans believed in Jesus because of the woman's testimony." The story of the Samaritan woman is an example of an author using seven items to demonstrate "step progression." The highlight is at the end of the list of seven (John 4:29).

John's Passion Story illustrates the use of seven items in "concentric arrangement" similar to the musical device employed by Bach. The technique of concentric composition was popular among ancient authors. In concentric composition, the main point of the narrative comes not at the end, but rather in the middle. When seven items are arranged concentrically, they appear thus:

A
  B
    C
      D
    C'
  B'
A'

John 18:1 to 19:41, the gospel reading for Good Friday, is like a play that can be divided into twenty-one scenes, or three acts each containing seven scenes. This means that the scenes of each act can be arranged according to the scheme of letters as presented just above. The "D" scene at the center is the highlight.

ACT 1 (18:1-27): Arrest, Jesus before Annas, denial by Peter

A Scene 1 (18:1) In the garden
  B Scene 2 (18:2-3) Infidelity of Judas
    C Scene 3 (18:4-11) Jesus loses none given to him; double witness
      D Scene 4 (18:12-14) transition from Judas to PETER; one must die
    C' Scene 5 (18:15-18) Peter's first denial, outside
  B' Scene 6 (18:19-24) Jesus and Annas: Teacher and Revealer; Jesus is struck, inside
A' Scene 7 (18:25-27) Peter's second and third denial, outside

ACT 2 (18:28–19:16): Jesus before Pilate.

To discern the scene changes here, pay attention to "inside" and "outside."

A Scene 1 (18:28-32): OUTSIDE, authorities demand death
  B Scene 2 (18:33-38a): INSIDE, Pilate questions, Jesus answers
    C Scene 3 (18:38b-40): OUTSIDE, Jesus declared innocent
      D Scene 4 (19:1-3): INSIDE, JESUS CROWNED AS KING
    C' Scene 5 (19:4-8): OUTSIDE, Jesus is declared innocent
  B' Scene 6 (19:9-12): INSIDE, Pilate questions, Jesus answers
A' Scene 7 (19:13-16): OUTSIDE, authorities demand death

Notice how section "D" is the heart of what John the Evangelist wants to say about Jesus in his Passion Story. Observe also how neatly the idea in section A matches the idea in section A', etc. Because of the literary device of "concentric arrangement," the reader (and sometimes a listener sensitive to this potential pattern) can easily grasp what the author or speaker is doing.

ACT 3 (19:17-42): Crucifixion; anointing; burial.

A Scene 1 (19:17-22) Crucifixion of Jesus, Pilate affirms twice
   B Scene 2 (19:23-24) Jesus stripped of clothing
      C Scene 3 (19:25-27) Jesus' mother affirms
         D Scene 4 (19:28-30) DEATH OF JESUS
      C' Scene 5 (19:31-37) Piercing of Jesus; double witness
   B' Scene 6 (19:38-40) Anointing of Jesus; fidelity of disciples
A' Scene 7 (19:41-42) Burial in a garden.

If one were to take a longer view of John's Passion Story, Act 1, scene 1 (in a garden), matches Act 3, scene 7 (in a garden), and so on, highlighting still further the centrality of Act 2 and its central scene: D.

This kind of literary arrangement makes it clear that the crowning of Jesus as king, the mocking indignity of the thorns endured out of love for humankind, is the key to the suffering and death of Jesus in the mind of John. Death out of love for others is victory; the cross in this scheme is indeed coronation.

The soldiers mock Jesus as "king." This practice of mockery was common on stage and in the Roman circuses. A "mock king" game has also been found on the stone pavement identified in John's gospel as *lithostrotos* (Greek for stone pavement) and located under the present Sisters of Zion convent in Jerusalem. In his Gospel John betrays a fondness for irony wherein protagonists often speak the truth totally unbeknown to themselves. In this perspective, here is a sign that non-Judaic peoples will ultimately confess the kingship of Jesus.

What would a Mediterranean cultural perspective add to this? In the Mediterranean world where honor and shame are the core values, Jesus the honorable preacher had a very shameful end. His trial and execution were that of a criminal. The shame of this end obliterated the honor he amassed during his ministry. This, at least, is the synoptic story line in which Jesus' being raised from the dead by God vindicates Jesus and heaps abundant honor upon him far surpassing anything humans could have granted.

In John, Jesus is honorable from the cosmic beginning of the Gospel right through the triumphalist trial and death. From a Mediterranean honor and shame perspective, the resurrection was something like frosting on the cake in John's Gospel. It simply added more honor to honor which was never diminished.

This is a comforting thought for a worshiper who, as this Good Friday liturgy progresses, will venerate the cross while singing or listening to the "reproaches," an Eastern hymn transferred to the West around the ninth century. The ceremony of venerating the cross was in existence in Rome from the seventh century. These "reproaches" represent the finest elements of folk piety calculated to prick the conscience and stir the hearts of sinners to conversion. St. Methodius, who brought Christianity to Poland in the ninth century A.D., also brought these "reproaches," which have held a treasured place in Polish piety through the ages even to the present time.

Isaiah 52:13–53:12

Modern specialists in Isaiah have preferred to reintegrate these Servant hymns into the total book rather than separate them out as individual "songs." In addition, modern scholarship believes that the traditional identification of the speaker in these hymns, "Suffering Servant," should rather be called "the faithful servant who willingly suffers." Scholars further believe that in Isaiah, the servant is not an individual but rather

Israel herself in history, captive Israel who will recognize herself in this persecuted sick person.

Israel the servant is described in Isaiah 1:4-6 (NAB):

> Ah, sinful nation,
>   a people laden with wickedness . . .
> The whole head is sick,
>   and the whole heart faint
> From the sole of the foot to the head
>   there is no sound spot;
> Wound and welt and gaping gash,
>   not drained, or bandaged,
> or eased with salve.

Isaiah's message in today's reading is that Israel, shattered, captive, and utterly humiliated will be restored. Israel has suffered for the same Israel who has sinned. The current state of humiliation is due to the fact that Isaiah's Israel is one with the Israel of history. Isaiah proposes that God regarded Israel's suffering, which God brought about, as some sort of offering for sin.

Today's liturgy as well as a long-standing Christian tradition reflected already in the Gospels applies this and its related passages to Jesus. It makes good cultural sense that the followers of Jesus would search their tradition for cultural heroes with whom they would associate and compare Jesus. Again, the sensitive preacher and liturgy planners will be careful in identifying "promise and fulfillment" patterns and will resist using these patterns in a "supercessionistic" sense.

The Hebrew Scripture stands quite well on its own with continued significance for Jewish believers of contemporary times. Judaism did not collapse after Jesus. But it is also proper for Christians to draw upon the Hebrew Scriptures to interpret Jesus the Galilean. This, it seems, is the intent of today's liturgy especially in the light of the revised references to Judaic people in the bidding prayers.

Hebrews 4:14-16; 5:7-9

In this meditation upon the significance of Jesus and his saving deed, the author of Hebrews notes that Christ the unique High Priest accomplished what the elaborate sacrificial Israelite ritual could not. He is an intercessor after the pattern of Abraham and Moses indeed, but very much more effective.

Pay special attention to the verses from Hebrews 5, for they were selected as especially suitable for Good Friday. These verses fit well with the sentiments of the Servant passage from Isaiah selected for today. They help a contemporary Western believer to shape an authentic image of a Mediterranean hero, someone Mediterranean boys would admire and emulate.

"*Precisely because* he was son, Jesus learned obedience from what he suffered. [Notice that I render this verse differently than it appears in traditional translations. See the explanation below.] He offered prayers and supplication with loud cries and tears to God, who was able to save him from death, and he was heard because of his reverence." The Passion Narratives tell us Jesus prayed for his Father to remove his cup of suffering, but concluded: "Your will not mine be done."

Now relate these sentiments to the repeated and emphatic exhortations in Proverbs (13:24; 19:18; 22:15; 23:13-14; 29:15, 17) and Ben Sira (30:1-13) that fathers should physically punish their sons. The image resulting from these segments of the Old Testament is shocking to a Westerner. What American father physically punishes his sons? What American father would will a shameful and violent death for his son? What American son would hang around and submit to it?

A Westerner wonders why Jesus does not flee or strive to extricate himself from this predicament? The answer is simple. Stoic endurance of pain and even death among males is highly admired and highly regarded in Mediterranean culture. Jesus was very much a man of his culture. It is reasonable to expect that Joseph and Mary followed the advice of Proverbs and Sirach in rearing Jesus, and it is reasonable to believe he read or heard and cherished Isaiah's passages about the faithful servant who suffered as well as the Lamentations of Jeremiah and the Psalms of Lament by various Israelite ancestors. These sentiments very plausibly comforted him on the cross where he hung from the third hour to the ninth before shrieking. The pagan Centurion expressed deep admiration for the *way he died*—like a real Mediterranean man (Mark 15:39)!

Today's readings from Hebrews and Isaiah give us an opportunity to understand and appreciate our ancestors in the faith on their own terms. We ought not be shocked or ashamed. They are, after all, our ancestors. We are grateful for what they tell us for it gives us a better understanding of Jesus as well. While we welcome the salvation Jesus won for us and admire the way in which it was gained, our culture holds a different set of values relative to pain and suffering. We are able not only to assuage physical pain and suffering but also to eliminate it. This God-given ability poses new challenges to the notion of "redemptive suffering." The mystery we celebrate today gives us much to think about.

Suggestions for the Homilist

The Scriptures assigned for today's liturgy offer the preacher at least two options. It is possible to go with John, adopt his triumphalist tone and emphasis on the divinity of Jesus, and anticipate Easter, as it were. We know Jesus died an ignominious death but it worked to our welfare. Let us celebrate!

The second option is to focus on pain and suffering, the suffering of innocent victims, and similar topics. This would provide an opportunity to explore cultural differences in experiencing and interpreting pain and suffering. There is a vast difference between the Mediterranean and Western views of pain and suffering. Preachers who choose this tack will quickly realize how vapid spiritualizing generalities are to Western believers who have at their disposal the marvels of cosmopolitan Western medicine. A terminally ill cancer patient responded to a sociologist's questionnaire in this way: "Three hours on the cross is easy; try a life-time of cancer!" The challenge will be to develop a suitable American stance toward suffering that has roots in the Judeo-Christian tradition but also respects modern, Western understanding. The preacher who successfully manages this challenge will serve the congregation very well.

Historical-Pastoral Reflections

The liturgical celebration of Good Friday was initiated as a historicization of a faith-festival mainly as a result of the establishment of Christianity as state religion in the fourth century. With Emperor Constantine's conversion, hordes of converts began to flock to the Church for baptism. These nominal Christians sorely needed to learn the gospel reports. The liturgy of Good Friday and the "original" Triduum (Friday, Saturday, and Easter Vigil) was a response to the catechetical needs of new converts to Christianity and the increased number of pilgrims to Jerusalem. How might the contemporary celebration of the Triduum meet contemporary catechetical needs of American believers?

1. The advances of scientific Western medicine have made it possible to eliminate physical pain and suffering, thus rendering them little more than a nuisance. This has serious implications for the traditional view of "redemptive suffering." How can preachers and liturgy planners help American worshipers to appreciate John's perspective on Jesus' passion and death?

2. Recent years have witnessed increased sensitivity of modern Christians toward modern Jews especially in regard to liturgical references. Consensus is building among biblical

scholars that the word "Jews" that appears so often in John's Gospel is an anachronistic English translation of Greek and Hebrew words: *ioudaioi; yehudim*. Both of these words should be translated *Judean*. This was the term used by "outsiders" (e.g., the Romans) to describe not only the inhabitants of Judea but of all ancient Palestine, and even those elsewhere in the world who worshiped the God whose temple was located in Jerusalem, in Judea. An alternate, historically appropriate term would be *Judaic people*. (See "Jews and Christians," pp. 98–104 in *The Cultural Dictionary of the Bible* [Collegeville: The Liturgical Press, 1999]). What steps might be taken in liturgical celebrations to obviate problems of anachronistic translations that might arise among non-Catholic visitors?

3. Further along these lines, the term "supercessionism" is a jargon word among scholars identifying an embarrassing tendency among some Christians to believe in general that the Old Testament has value only as it is fulfilled and surpassed in the New Testament. One can see traces of this even in the documents of Vatican II! What do Isaiah's songs of the faithful servant who suffers mean to contemporary Jewish worshipers? How does that compare with its meaning for contemporary Christians?

4. Contemporary political experiences in the Middle East provide vivid illustrations of Mediterranean values. Stoic suffering of pain taught through the physical disciplining of children is an abiding value in those cultures. This fusion of love and violence is reflected in the belief that "those whom God loves he chastises" (Prov 3:11-12; compare Heb 12:1-11). Books on childrearing written for American believers by fundamentalist Christians tend to endorse this "biblical" form of parenting. Does the reading from Hebrews for today's liturgy reflect a "biblical" or a "cultural" view? How can a reader distinguish these two viewpoints?

3

Easter Vigil

> **Readings:**
> Cycle A: Matthew 28:1-10
> Cycle B: Mark 16:1-8
> Cycle C: Luke 24:1-12
> Romans 6:3-11
> Genesis 1:1–2:2
> Genesis 22:1-18
> Exodus 14:15–15:1
> Isaiah 54:5-14
> Isaiah 55:1-11
> Baruch 3:9-15, 32–4:4
> Ezekiel 36:16-28

Cycle A: Matthew 28:1-10

Matthew's account is the closest any of the Scripture passages comes to describing the actual resurrection of Jesus. He highlights the descent of an angel who rolls the stone away from the tomb-opening, and then sits on the stone. From a symbolic perspective, when it sealed the tomb, the stone signified death's victory; rolled back, it signifies victory over death.

The angel announces to the women that Jesus has been raised. The verb "has been raised" is in the passive voice. (The preacher may have to help the congregation distinguish passive voice from past tense.) This means that the subject of the sentence is the recipient rather than the performer of the action expressed by the verb. Somebody "raised" Jesus up. In the Bible the unnamed somebody who performs the action of verbs in the passive voice is generally understood to be God if no human agent is in sight.

The passive voice in the Greek language of the New Testament allowed our ancestors in the faith to speak about God without mentioning the deity's name at all. This was an especially valuable grammatical strategy for Judaic converts who accepted Jesus as Messiah and who routinely substituted the Hebrew word "Lord" for the name of God wherever it occurred in the Hebrew Bible. Modern scholars call these verb forms "theological passives" because they point to God as the unnamed doer of the action described by the verb. Thus our ancestors in the faith who heard or read the sentence: "Jesus has been raised" would automatically complete the sentence in their minds: "by God, of course."

Other examples of the "theological passive": "knock and it shall be opened for you" (by God, of course; Matt 7:7); "Blessed are those who mourn for they shall be comforted" (by God, of course; Matt 5:4); the petitions of the Our Father: "may your name be hallowed" (by you, God; Matt 6:9), and many more.

True to his penchant for emphasizing prophetic fulfillment, Matthew adds a distinctive comment: "as he promised." Readers familiar with Matthew's Gospel recognize that fulfillment of prophecy is a favorite theme of this evangelist (see 12:40; 16:20; 17:23; 20:19; 25:32).

Of the Gospels assigned for the Easter Vigil in each cycle, only Matthew reports an appearance of Jesus (vv. 9-10). Mary Magdalene and the other Mary see the risen Jesus who directs them to "Go and carry the news to my brothers." Jesus thus makes them apostles to the apostles. Jesus' reference to his

apostles as "brothers" suggests that they are forgiven for aban-
doning him in his darkest hour.

The fact that Jesus seems to repeat to the women the same
message they just heard from the angel is interpreted by some
scholars as indicating that Matthew has either created these
verses or compacted the appearance of Jesus to Mary Magdalene reported in John 20:11-18. Whichever interpretation one
selects, it is fair to ask: what was Matthew's purpose in presenting this appearance? It seems very likely that he wanted to
highlight the women's response to the risen Jesus as the proper
response from all believers: they approach and worship him
(see Matt 21:1-12; 28:16-20).

It is interesting to note that in Rabbinic tradition, the testimony of women is discountable. Yet Christian tradition holds
firmly to an appearance by the risen Jesus to women. This "ir-
regularity" is precisely the kind of information that argues for
the facticity and "historicity" (this is a difficult word to use; it
needs careful explanation) of the report about Jesus' resurrection. If the resurrection of Jesus were imagined or created by
devoted followers who were frustrated by their leader's sudden
and shameful death, logic dictates that they should create a
perfect scenario with legitimate events and acceptable witnesses. But "witnesses" of what?

No one witnessed the event. Everyone who wanted to
could go and inspect an empty tomb. What did the empty tomb
mean? A number of explanations are possible: (1) the women
went to the wrong tomb; (2) the disciples stole the body and
created a story of Jesus' resurrection and appearances; (3)
Jesus only seemed to die; in truth he revived and wandered
away; (4) Jesus was raised from the dead.

Matthew focuses on two of these explanations. He claims
that the theft hypothesis was concocted by the chief priests and
guards at the tomb (28:11-15), and "this story has been spread
among the Judaic people to this [Matthew's] day" (Matt
28:15). The only other explanation of the empty tomb for

Matthew is that Jesus was raised by God. This is the announcement of the angel and the risen Jesus to the women.

Lending credence to these announcements are the many
witness reports of appearances of the risen Jesus. Appearance
stories, such as that reported by Matthew, are a necessary con-
comitant to the fact of the empty tomb. Other gospel accounts
about "witnesses" to appearances include Luke 24; John 20–21;
and Mark 16:9-20. Paul's report of early Christian tradition re-
counts still other appearances: "to Cephas, then to the twelve.
Then he appeared to more than five hundred brethren at one time,
most of whom are still alive, though some have fallen asleep.
Then he appeared to James, then to all the apostles. Last of all, as
to one untimely born, he appeared also to me" (1 Cor 15:5-8).

Many of these reports emphasize that these appearances
were not hallucinations, visions, dreams, or any other such
thing. The risen Jesus eats and drinks ordinary fare; he is not
invisible nor a ghost. In truth, these are real experiences of
Jesus in alternate reality. The experiences take place in altered
states of consciousness which are common and ordinary
among 90 percent of the people on the face of this planet today
and an even greater percentage in antiquity. (See "alternate reality," pp. 81–84 in my *The Cultural Dictionary of the Bible*
[Collegeville: The Liturgical Press, 1999].)

Thus, if the tomb is empty, and witnesses experiencing altered states of consciousness have seen the risen Jesus alive in
alternate realty, then he has been raised by God indeed! This and
the continued growth and development of the Church are the
rock solid foundation of Christian faith in Jesus' resurrection.

Cycle B: Mark 16:1-8

This original and brief ending to Mark's Gospel tells
God's greatest work: Jesus has been raised (v. 6)! There is no
appearance of Jesus here, only an empty tomb and an announcement by a heavenly messenger. The significance of the

announcement is usually very difficult for Americans to grasp. The announcement requires an appreciation for the rules of grammar, something which is not a strong suit with Americans. (See the explanation above for Matthew.)

The first hearers or readers of Mark's Gospel, the majority of whom would not have been eye-witnesses of the risen Jesus, were reminded and assured that faith, conversion, and discipleship depend not on resurrection appearances but on the word of promise.

The significance of this favorite grammatical structure among our ancestors in the faith is that it meshes so well with their Mediterranean culture. In this world, human beings prefer "being" (= spontaneous and unreflective responses to any cue) to "doing" (= carefully planned activity calculated to achieve a purpose). God does all the "doing," while his creatures respond spontaneously to whatever God does ("being"). One reason why Americans experience difficulty understanding passive voice is because of the American cultural preference for "doing" over "being." Passivity is not an American value. Americans are uneasy just hanging out, hanging loose, simply waiting. They must act and get it over with.

This same insight helps a Western reader to appreciate the behavior of the messenger and the women in Mark's story of the empty tomb. Since it is mainly God and his supra-human creatures who are major "doers" in Mediterranean understanding, heavenly messengers are routine experiences in that world. People who communicate with God and other spirits do so in an altered state of consciousness. After all, the deity and other spirits inhabit alternate reality. Even so, encountering God or a heavenly messenger in our reality—material reality—is always astonishing (see Exod 3:3; Isa 6:1-5; Jer 1:6-8; Ezek 1:28; Luke 1:29-30). The messenger therefore seeks to settle the nerves of people to whom he appears by saying: "Fear not," or "Please don't be astonished or amazed," or the like (Mark 16:6). Normal, Mediterranean human reaction is indeed astonishment (16:6), reverence or trembling and ecstasy (16:8), and speechlessness (16:8) as a result of this close encounter with the supra-human world.

This cultural background supports a positive interpretation of this gospel passage, such as that offered by the Passion Narrative specialist, Fr. Donald Senior:

> The women at the tomb encountered the living word of God and finally glimpsed the awesome mystery of the Kingdom. Now they flee from the tomb on their mission, trembling and in ecstasy. What they have seen is unutterable, transcending all human hope. They therefore leave in fear, gripped by the same wondrous awe that had stunned biblical witnesses from Moses to Paul. The fearful and resplendent presence of the living God was now seen as never before in the crucified Messiah's victory over death (Donald Senior, C.P., *The Passion of Jesus in the Gospel of Mark* [Wilmington, Del.: Michael Glazier, Inc., 1984] 137).

Even so, some scholars prefer to interpret the shock of Matt 16:8 as presenting a negative example. Christian believers ought not to follow the example of these frightened women who fail just like the disciples have failed. In this interpretation, the ending is seen as an effort to purge the fear in the Markan community associated with preaching the Gospel.

Experienced contemporary preachers already know that where there are two scripture scholars, there are three opinions! The preacher will certainly present the opinion that most resonates with personal faith but may also choose to present the congregation with other options as well.

Cycle C: Luke 24:1-12

Luke's distinctive resurrection report is the story of a single day. Everything happened on this "first day of the week": resurrection, appearances of Jesus, and the ascension. The verses read at the vigil recount only the discovery of the empty tomb and a meeting with "two men." This event is yet another instance of an experience by human beings who have entered an altered state of consciousness. The gleaming white robes of the men is characteristic of such an experience. The two men ask a question and make an announcement:

> Why do you seek the living among the dead? [He is not here, but has been raised!] Remember how he told you, while he was still in Galilee, that the Son of man must be delivered into the hands of sinful men, and be crucified, and on the third day rise.

The significance of the announcement is rooted in an appreciation for the rules of grammar. The passive voice indicates God raised Jesus from the dead. The first hearers or readers of Luke's Gospel, the majority of whom would not have been eye-witnesses of the Risen Jesus (like those in the gospel reports), were reminded and assured that faith, conversion, and discipleship depend not on resurrection appearances but on the word of promise. If an envoy from God reports that God did something, why should the recipient require further confirmation?

Clearly, this proclamation: "He is not here, but has been raised" is the heart of this scene at the empty tomb. The heavenly messengers have given this message first to pious, observant Judaic women. Then they are reminded of what he told them while he was still in Galilee. Luke alone among the Evangelists makes this reference to Jesus' predictions of his death and resurrection. The women then take the report back to the Eleven, but the men did not believe the women. Their report did not give birth to faith. Indeed, the Eleven viewed the stories "as an idle tale" or "nonsense" as the NAB renders it.

It is well for scientifically oriented Americans to keep in mind that resurrection in Christian faith does not mean that a corpse returns to life. Lazarus who was in the tomb four days returned to life, but the event is not described as a "resurrection." Nor does the Christian faith believe that a body bereft

temporarily of a soul eventually rejoins it. Such "Greek" philo-
sophical thinking (body and soul) had not yet fully permeated
the Mediterranean world. What is key to the concrete Palestin-
ian Judaic way of thinking is the *transformation* of the person
in risen life. People who knew Jesus in his earthly life did not
immediately recognize him in risen life, as he is in alternate reality. This is surely the experience of the disciples on the road
to Emmaus (Luke 24:13-35).

In 1984, Pheme Perkins, the Boston College biblical
scholar wrote: "The theological task of articulating the significance of resurrection for twentieth-century Christians still re-
mains to be undertaken" (*Resurrection*, Doubleday, 30). This
may be a small consolation to contemporary preachers and
liturgy planners in the twenty-first century, but none should
shrink from the challenge of making a fresh attempt. Interpreting the resurrection appearances as altered states of consciousness (ASC) experiences of Jesus in alternate reality places the
discussion in a new context. This kind of experience is very
similar to that of other people in the contemporary world who
have ASC experiences of recently deceased persons. Medical
and anthropological literature provide many examples.

Romans 6:3-11

In Romans 5–8 Paul highlights God's love and exhorts
the Roman Christians to "consider yourselves dead to sin and
alive to God in Christ Jesus" (6:11). The singular "sin" is important. Paul is not talking about human failing of some sort.
Rather his Greek word for sin is more correctly understood as
a force or a power that drives a person toward an almost un-
avoidable proneness to failure or to committing an evil deed.
Remember that Mediterranean culture views human beings as
subject to nature rather than as controlling nature. Nature, in
the Mediterranean world, includes an invisible world of pow-
ers and forces which mischievously, capriciously, or some-

times even with deliberate calculation intervene in human life and cause human beings to behave in ways that displease God. This world of power and forces is the context in which Paul understands sin.

The good news in Paul's passage is that Jesus' death and resurrection has destroyed the effectiveness of this force or power called sin. Furthermore, baptism snatches believers from the power of this force and incorporates them into new life with God. This is something very real and welcome in the Mediterranean way of thinking. While some people in this world use amulets, gestures, or incantations to ward off evil, Christians through baptism are intimately united with the very one who has defeated the source of all evil.

But people still fail and commit sins. It is to this situation that Paul speaks when he exhorts the Romans: since thanks to baptism our old self was crucified (v. 6) and we are now "alive to God in Christ Jesus" (v. 11), we should live accordingly.

This reading is quite obviously appointed for the Easter Vigil because of the current practice permitting the administration of baptism during the ceremonies. Historically, as Thomas Talley notes, baptism at Alexandria before the Council of Nicea appears to have been administered on the Saturday before Palm Sunday so as not to interfere with the celebration of the Triduum.

Whether or not candidates will be baptized at a given celebration of the Easter Vigil, the preacher should likely take the opportunity to reflect on this sacrament and its current place in the celebration of the Lord's resurrection.

Though familiar to worshipers from catechetics and preaching, this basic Christian belief about the relationship of baptism with the death and resurrection of Jesus is often unimpressive and unconvincing to American believers. In the American mind nature exists to be tamed, harnessed, and controlled. Spirits, good and bad, are by and large unscientific superstitions. Americans know the difference between good and evil, and feel perfectly free and capable of choosing one or the other. Such thinking coexists quite comfortably with the widespread popular belief in angels.

Preachers to American congregations face the challenge of helping Americans transfer their focus from individual sins and sinful actions (plural) to sin (singular) as our ancestors in the faith understood it: a force that drives a person irresistibly toward individual evil deeds. While not the same thing, habits and addictions, which are realities very familiar to Americans, can help them appreciate what our ancestors in the faith viewed as an irresistible power or force. It is precisely this from which our ancestors felt saved and redeemed. Americans would likely consider freedom from unwanted habits and addictions a blessing, too.

THE VIGIL READINGS

Of the seven readings proposed for the vigil, many congregations read at least four and sometimes five! A well-paced and prayerful reading of the texts and the responses sung by the congregation can help create a reflective atmosphere for the rest of the liturgy. The following insights may contribute to a richer appreciation of these familiar readings.

Genesis 1:1–2:2

In the Mediterranean world boys and girls are reared together up until the age of puberty by the women. Boys are routinely and regularly pampered, including the fact that they are breast-fed at least twice as long as girls are and often long after they have learned to speak (see 2 Macc 7:27). The male child soon learns that all he need do is say "milk" or "food," and he will be fed. Early in life Mediterranean people recognize the power of a word.

Additionally from this childhood experience of pampering, adult Mediterranean males develop an aversion to manual, or specifically hand-soiling, labor. Thus, from personal experience, all Mediterranean people take it for granted that God could create the universe by simply saying "Let there be . . . ." Words are powerful and effective. Moreover, in this version of the creation story, God does not even soil his hands! Surely God can do what any Mediterranean man can do.

Genesis 22:1-18

At the age of puberty, the Mediterranean boy is unceremoniously and forcefully pushed out of the women's world to take his proper, hierarchical place in the male world. This shocking experience causes him to run back to the women, who must continue to expel him from their company. Having had little contact with men to this point, the boy experiences a gender-identity crisis. What does it mean to be a man? How ought a man behave?

In Mediterranean culture males distinguish themselves by an ability to bear physical pain without flinching. Fathers initiate their adolescent sons into bearing pain. Later, the grown sons initiate their sons into bearing pain, and the cycle continues. Proverbs (13:24; 19:18; 22:15; 23:13-14; 29:15, 17) and Ben Sira (30:1-13) contain more than one exhortation to fathers to physically punish their son if they hope for an honorable adult.

These notions help a modern reader understand the story of a seemingly docile Isaac in the face of a terrifying ordeal about to be dealt to him by his father. One contemporary author of Mediterranean ancestry expresses this cultural ideal thus: "In a fight, I would never give up or say 'enough,' even though the other were killing me. I would try to go to my death, smiling. That is what we mean by being 'macho'" (Oscar Lewis, *Children of Sanchez*). Isaac may not have been smiling as he faced death, but an American believer wonders why he didn't overpower his father or simply run away?

Child sacrifice in the Bible is noted in 2 Kgs 3:27; Jer 7:31; Ezek 16:20; and forbidden in Exod 13:15; Deut 12:29-

31; and 1 Kgs 16:34. The Isaac story may represent an earlier stage of tradition that legitimated the substitution of an animal for child sacrifice. The present version of the story suggests (in v. 5) that Abraham recognized that this was only a test of his loyalty to God. He tells the servant: "I and the boy will return . . ." Even though frightened, Abraham and the boy remained faithfully obedient.

In the context of today's celebration, God was satisfied with Abraham's willingness. Isaac did not actually have to be sacrificed after all. Jesus too was willing to suffer, but his Father did not let the cup pass from him. For many believers, their experience is more like Jesus' than Isaac's experience.

Exodus 14:15–15:1

In the first-century Mediterranean world, more than 90 percent of the population were peasants. They regularly experienced scarcity and realized their inability to help themselves. Those few who could help were known as "patrons," while the needy were known as "clients." Sometimes an intermediary acted like a "broker" between a patron and clients. It is this cultural imagery that our ancestors in the faith utilized for understanding God.

God was the patron of the Israelites, and Moses was a broker between God and the Israelite clients. God the patron resolved to free his Israelite clients from Egyptian bondage with the aid of Moses his broker. But when the clients saw the Egyptians hot on their trail, they doubted the abilities of God and Moses, their patron and the appointed broker.

Insisting on using Moses as the broker (vv. 16-17), God promises to bring destruction upon the Egyptians. From this God will "get glory or honor over Pharaoh." And when Israel saw that God the patron can deliver on the divine promises, they "feared (= respected) the Lord" and regained their trust in the patron (God) and the broker (Moses, vv. 30-31).

In successful patronage, everybody wins. The client (Israel) gets that which is needed and which cannot be obtained anywhere else or can't be obtained on such beneficial terms. The patron (God) gets honor, which is the main reason why anyone bothers to become a patron at all. And the patron's broker (Moses) either regains or gains an increase in credibility as one who can facilitate the deal with the patron.

When the patron delivers, the Mediterranean client must pay for the gift received. The payment consists in singing the patron's praise, that is, broadcasting far and wide the honor of the patron. Hence the very logical canticle that Moses and the Israelites sing immediately, spontaneously, and quite publicly to the Lord. That is what honor is about.

Isaiah 54:5-14

Honor and shame are the core or driving values behind Mediterranean culture. Men are associated with honor, and women are associated with shame mainly because they are most vulnerable to attacks on their man's (father's, brother's, or husband's) honor. When a man fails to chisel away at another man's honor rating or honor claim directly, that man will attack the other man's women. Sometimes the woman initiates waywardness and subjects her males (father, brother, or husband) to shame.

In either case, the shamed man responsible for guarding and protecting this now sullied women has two options: an honorable one—be rid of the unfaithful spouse; or a shameful one—overlook the woman's failing and take her back.

In the Mediterranean world the ideal marriage partner is a first cousin (one's father's brother's daughter). But if this marriage partner proves unfaithful, the honorable husband will first see if another proper partner, a cousin, is available. If no other suitable partner is available, the honorable husband may swallow his shame. What good will it do to destroy a faithless

wife and end up a life-long widower? Better to bear the shame
of taking back a wayward wife and exercise greater vigilance
in the future than do the right thing, get rid of the wife, and remain single for the rest of life.

This makes excellent Mediterranean human sense. But
God chose Israel from among many nations and can surely
find another nation to love. First-cousin considerations don't
enter here. That God would take back a wayward partner is
shocking news to Mediterranean folk. A God who would do
this does not behave honorably, at least not as humans understand honor. Such a God is like a cuckold! (Adultery is a common image for Israel's lack of loyalty to God.)

That such behavior could be considered compassionate or
merciful would stretch this cultural imagination quite a bit. Yet
that appears to be precisely Isaiah's intention! Isn't that the
function prophets play on behalf of the Lord? Thus the prophet
draws upon this culturally uncharacteristic marriage behavior
to assure Israel that God will indeed forget her "shame" and re-
pair their mutual relationship that was disturbed by the Exile.
Good news for faithless Israel! Astonishing behavior by God!

Salvation from the tragedy of Exodus and Exile. What a
powerful patron God is!

Isaiah 55:1-11

Nothing in the Mediterranean world is free, even though
money is rarely involved. An invitation received and accepted
is an obligation that must be repaid. Reciprocity is what makes
the economic world go round in the ancient world. Here, however, Second Isaiah concludes his consoling message (chs.
41–55) by inviting all to the banquet of God's joy, but he also
insists that God declines the reciprocal return. In the Middle
East, if you accept an invitation to a meal you are obliged to return the favor. People who lacked this capability would ordi-
narily turn down the invitation. Isaiah says that even if you

have no money, that is, if you do not have the wherewithal to reciprocate as expected, come to the banquet anyway. The only real requirement is to heed the Lord and/or seek the Lord. This is a small price to pay in order to eat well at a banquet featuring rich fare.

That the prophet was quite aware of presenting God in another culturally shocking posture is evident from the words attributed to the Lord in verse 8: Shocked are you? surprised? amazed? "My ideas and activities are significantly different from yours!"

A modern believer is forced to admire the prophet's efforts to meet the challenge of explaining to God's people in exile that God really wants to re-establish his "covenant of peace" (Isa 54:10) or the "everlasting covenant" assured to David (Isa 55:3). They are now in Babylon as a result of a broken covenant. At first this seemed tragic, but within the fifty years of exile these displaced Judeans have prospered and fared well. With everything going so well in Babylon, why would these exiles want to return to the unwalled and demolished city of Jerusalem? The prophet has a hard sell on his hands.

Baruch 3:9-15, 32–4:4

Attributed to Jeremiah's secretary and companion, Baruch, this book is a pastiche of biblical passages drawn from Daniel 9, Job 28, and Isaiah 40–66. Baruch is definitely not the author. In fact there may be as many as four authors of this book, and internal evidence suggests dating it somewhere between 200 to 60 B.C., the Maccabean period.

The particular poem selected for this liturgy reflects the largely secular wisdom tradition of the Bible whose themes are the elusive nature of wisdom and an identification of wisdom with the Torah or Law. Scant mention is made of the Exile, and there is no extended reflection on it. Nevertheless, the entire book of Baruch and this, its central poem, offer a reflection on various aspects of Israel's exile in Babylon.

According to Baruch, God, the fountain of Wisdom, has revealed life's true meaning and purpose to Jacob and Israel. If Israel would be faithful to God's commandments, she would experience peace and long life. True wisdom is found in God's gift of the Torah, the Law.

The author's concluding verses sum up his enthusiasm quite well:

> Give not your honor to another,
>> your privileges to an alien race,
> Blessed are we, O Israel;
>> For we really know what pleases God! (NAB adapted)

Ezekiel 36:16-28

The standard prophetic preaching invariably stresses the necessity of conversion and repentance as well as the resolve to remain righteous if Israelite exiles expect to return to the land (see Ezek 18; 33). In this oracle, however, God behaves according to the pattern of standard Mediterranean patronage, pure and simple.

At issue is honor, the honor of the God who is Israel's patron. By turning to idolatry, these clients behaved shamefully toward God their patron. As any insulted patron would, God drops his clients like hot potatoes. Worse, God the patron takes vengeance for his experience of dishonor by causing them to be scattered into exile!

But here in exile, non-Israelites comment: "These are the people of the Lord? yet they had to leave their land?" (Ezek 36:20) Non-Israelites laugh at a patron who was unable to look after the security of personal clients. God the patron is now subject to ridicule and shame rather than the scoundrel clients! No patron has to put up with this kind of ridicule and shame, and neither does God. So God acts NOT primarily in the interests of the clients but rather in genuine self interest out of concern for the honor that was tarnished: "It is not for your sake, Israel, that I act, but for my sake, for my honor which you have tarnished among the nations. And I will restore my honor. And the nations will know that I am a decent and effective patron, I am the Lord."

God does two things: God removes the wayward clients from exile, thereby regaining personal honor as an effective patron. Second, God recreates the clients by giving a new heart and a new spirit so that henceforth the behavior of God's clients will be a credit to their patron. God renews the patronage contract: "You shall be my clients, and I will be your patron—you shall be my people, and I will be your God!" (Ezek 26:28) Please note well the one-sidedness of patronage: the patron takes the initiative, the patron seeks and selects the clients!

Suggestions for Homilists

The gospels and epistle for the vigil Mass proper present an opportunity to emphasize the fact that faith and discipleship which are a consequence of baptism (Romans) do not rest on proof, but on trusting in the word (Mark; Luke) and in the appearances of Jesus which render the empty tomb a testimony to Jesus' resurrection (Matthew).

What unified story do the seven vigil readings tell? From one perspective they summarize God's wonderful works on behalf of the covenant people and the people's respective responses throughout history. From another perspective, these readings describe God's various covenants (for example, Adamic, Abrahamic, Mosaic, Davidic, Ezekiel's) or covenant allusions (mention of the exile in terms of broken marriage [Isaiah] or forgetting the Torah [Baruch]).

Undergirding all of these reflections are various elements of Mediterranean culture. All theology is analogy, which means that everything human beings think and say about God is rooted in human experience. The Scripture reflections about God are rooted in Mediterranean human experience and reflect that culture admirably well. Honor and shame, patronage, honorable way of being a father—these are some key cultural elements involved in the vigil readings. Without these Mediterranean cultural insights, words like sin, salvation, redemption, covenant, and the like remain little more than theological jargon.

Historical-Pastoral Reflections

1. Discuss the power of language; reflect on the significance of the "theological passive" voice of the verb in New Testament Greek. Bill Clinton, Ronald Reagan, and George Bush, among other politicians, have taught us how even the English language can be manipulated so as to pass off painful, undesirable, or shameful experiences as innocuous or innocent. Do preachers and liturgy planners pay sufficient attention to the power of language in the liturgy? in selecting and declaiming Scripture readings for the liturgy? Do cantors and leaders of prayer respect and utilize the power of antiphons, responses, and the like?

2. Reflect upon the rich symbolism of the Easter Vigil liturgy: fire, water, darkness, light, death, and life. Explore how to allow each of these symbols to speak even louder than the words of the liturgy.

3. Make a list of the theological or liturgical jargon words commonly used in regard to Holy Week and the Triduum:

> sin
> salvation
> redemption
> redemptive suffering
> covenant
> atonement
> resurrection

and then review the elements of Mediterranean culture listed below that have been highlighted in this series of reflections:

> honor
> shame
> Mediterranean men
> Mediterranean women
> Mediterranean ways of being a father or mother
> physical punishment and suffering joined with love (the fusion of love and violence)
> patronage
> clientelism
> sin as force or power

Can you draw up a list of distinctive American cultural interests and concerns relative to Holy Week and the Triduum?

How can a preacher and the liturgical planners bridge these various cultures in planning "meaningful liturgies" for their congregations?

4

Easter Sunday

Readings:
John 20:1-9
Acts 10:34, 37-43
Colossians 3:1-4
or 1 Corinthians 5:6-8

John 20:1-9

The gospel for Easter Sunday presents another version of the empty tomb discovery which was also featured at the Easter Vigil. In John's version, the tomb is found empty by Mary and then visited by Peter and John. Mary is clearly grief-stricken by the suspicion that perhaps the authorities have removed Jesus' body from the tomb as a final hostile act of further shaming his reputation. Mary may be considered to represent the community's grief and need for consolation, though it cannot be denied that she also represents a concern in the community about a claim that Christians stole the body in order to manufacture a deception about Jesus rising from the dead.

A second underlying tradition appears to relate that Peter came to the tomb, looked in and saw nothing, but could not understand the significance of what he saw because he did not know the scriptural prophecy that Jesus would be raised from the dead.

In John's version of the empty tomb story, the Beloved Disciple looked in and "saw and believed" thus making his reaction the real climax to this account. What exactly did the Beloved Disciple see? Of course the same things Peter saw: an empty tomb and neatly folded grave clothes. The Beloved Disciple may have been more even-tempered than Peter and might have concluded that thieves or hostile authorities would not have removed the grave clothes or been so tidy in removing the body as to fold the grave clothes in a neat pile. His quick conclusion and firm belief was that Jesus was indeed raised!

Ambiguous and uneven though the various segments of this pericope may be, one fact stands out quite clearly. The earliest tradition of Jesus' resurrection was clearly rooted in the discovery of an empty tomb. The place where his body was laid is now empty, and the body is nowhere in sight. Today's selection from John's Gospel illustrates a variety of normal and very understandable human responses. At the same time, it points to the key for facing and unraveling the confusing evidence: the necessity of understanding the Scripture about Jesus!

Once again the preacher has an opportunity to remind worshipers that this New Testament tradition about the empty tomb serves to underscore the fact that faith comes through hearing the proclamation that the Lord is risen. In John's version of the empty tomb, there is no angelic proclamation to explain matters. Instead we have the testimony about the Beloved Disciple which appears to fulfill that function: he "saw and believed" and those who hear this account come to faith or increased faith in hearing it.

Acts 10:34a, 37-43

The speech crafted by Luke for Peter in this selection from Acts demonstrates how far Peter was able to progress in contrast to his initial dumbfounded response to the empty tomb he found in today's gospel. Even an intimate day-by-day companion of Jesus like Peter who began his faith-life at ground zero could ultimately draw on the very Scriptures he was once unable to fathom.

Perhaps because this speech represents the content of preaching to the non-Israelites rather than to Israelites, Peter does not use the "theological passive" construction which obviates the need to pronounce God's name ("Jesus was raised" by YHWH). Instead, Peter names the agent in a straightforward declarative sentence: "God raised him up on the third day!"

The speech itself summarizes Jesus' ministry, passion, death, and resurrection. Then it points out that witnesses or preachers were legitimated (chosen beforehand by God; commissioned to preach). And finally, the point of the speech: everyone who believes in Jesus has forgiveness of sins through his name.

In larger context of this speech, Luke is attempting to explain how it is that one does not have to become an Israelite first in order to enter the Messianist group which accepts Jesus as Messiah. He makes the point that God keeps promises made. God saves everyone who believes (better: all who are loyal!), and ordinary, good people are very pleasing and acceptable to God.

These explanations are very consoling to Messianists (Israelites who accept Jesus as Messiah) who are harassed for believing that the Messiah Jesus saves Israelites and non-Israelites alike, yet heartening to non-Israelites who accept Jesus without having to submit to circumcision. Thus does Luke draw out the implications of the significance of Jesus' death and resurrection. These are also the further implications of what the Beloved Disciple "believed" after what he "saw" in the empty tomb.

Colossians 3:1-4

A clever admirer of Paul who perfectly understood his hero's concepts made creative use of them in this letter written in Paul's name and addressed to late first-century believers living near Laodicea not far from Pammukale in what is now modern Turkey.

In this passage a Pauline disciple exhorts believers to be faithful to their dying and rising to new life in Christ. One must be careful here not to misinterpret the epistle. The exhortation to "set your minds on things that are above, not on things that are on earth" (v. 2) is not intended as an invitation to spurn the world and prefer the heavenly realm, or eschew materialism and prefer spirituality. This world is important. It is the place where human beings develop their life with God. The household-codes in 3:18–4:1 offer very down-to-earth advice on very mundane affairs: marriage, family, and work.

Life "in Christ" is a hidden reality not readily visible to ordinary vision. Nevertheless, Christians are obliged to develop this Christ-life in themselves, in their every-day world. Its full bloom will be revealed at the Parousia, the end-time appearance of Christ when believers will be united with him in full glory and honor.

1 Corinthians 5:6-8

In chapters 5–7 Paul addresses problems most likely communicated to him orally about utter sexual wantonness in Corinth, a city whose name in antiquity became synonymous with such license. The architects of the lectionary, however, have yanked these verses from context and thus both recreated the scripture and reinterpreted the selected verses.

In Paul's original scheme, these verses were intended to deflate the Corinthian "boasting" (v. 6a) about incestuous behavior (v. 1). He therefore gives a command (v. 7a: excommunicate the sinner!) and then provides a rationale for the behavior (v. 7b: Christ our paschal lamb has been sacrificed; incest is ungrateful behavior for the salvation worked by Christ). How should redeemed believers behave? "With sincerity and truth" regarding the salvation offered by Christ (v. 8)! Thus did Paul present his "theological justification" for excommunicating the man who was living with his stepmother in clear violation of Lev 18:8.

Torn from context and inserted into the Liturgy for Easter Sunday, Paul's solution for a specific place (Corinth) at a specific time (A.D. 54) becomes instead a general moralizing exhortation artificially linked with the celebration of the resurrection of Jesus. In the Israelite Passover, leaven is removed from the home before the feast. With Jesus' resurrection, the old leaven/sin must be removed after the fact!

On the other hand, the preacher who chooses this text for the celebration can restore Paul's original Corinthian context for the verses and use the passage to draw out still further implications of the gospel reading (Jesus is raised!) and the selection from Acts (what did Jesus accomplish for us?). The question for worshipers then becomes this: if one takes the kerygma seriously (John; Acts), one may have to make serious and far-reaching decisions! One may indeed have to remove the leaven.

Suggestions for Homilists

Major liturgical feasts like Easter and Christmas are difficult occasions on which to preach. In the United States, our secular culture has overlaid these religious feasts with equally impressive and competitive secular meaning and symbols. Worshipers sitting in the pews have very likely never attempted to separate and sort out the competing traditions and symbols.

The preacher who resorts to stock, theological jargon will certainly be orthodox but may not stir to conversion. Even

Mediterranean cultural insights might not be sufficiently effective to cut through to the heart of the message. The liturgical use/abuse of the Corinthian text as noted above might provide a fitting vehicle for a conscientious preacher to resist generalities and focus pointedly on the significance of this central event in Christian faith.

Historical-Pastoral Reflections

1. The two empty tomb scenes (Mark's at the Vigil; and John's for Easter Sunday) present an opportunity to highlight the Christian conviction that "Faith comes from hearing" the proclamation of the resurrection. How might this be accomplished at the Easter Sunday liturgy celebrated in all its festive solemnity?

2. The alternative reading from 1 Corinthians proposed for Easter Sunday offers an opportunity for the preacher and liturgy planning team to discuss the "liturgical use" of Scripture. Discuss the assigned reading as it is and also in terms of its context in 1 Corinthians. Catholics are repeatedly warned not to yank Scripture texts out of context, yet the liturgy not only does this with regularity but combines texts never intended to be so conjoined by their authors and thereby creates "new" Scripture! What are the pastoral implications of such "liturgical use" of Scripture?

NOTE: This is a difficult and thorny issue to discuss. Likely no conclusion will be reached in the discussion. Still it is worthwhile for the preacher and liturgy planners to reflect on the challenge periodically in order to keep their assumptions and convictions up front and honest.